a dream once lost

tia shearer bassett

Uproar Theatrics

LICENSING & PRODUCTION INQUIRIES
Uproar Theatrics, LLC.
hello@uproartheatrics.com | www.UproarTheatrics.com

a dream once lost previewed in Nashville and had its professional premiere at the Philly Fringe in 2007, directed by Matt Bassett.

The cast included:
Tia Shearer (sophi)
Marin Miller (attlea)
Phil Perry (star, counter-king, others)
Evelyn Blythe (star, queen, aychpot, others)
Robert Marigza (star, emory, child, others)

Designed and supported by:
Jordan Lehning (original scoring)
Lauren Sandidge (costumes)
H.T. Rader (props)
Matt Bassett (sound)
Taylor Jones (stage manager)

Special thanks to the Woodmont Ave. First Unitarian Universalist Church community for championing the piece, and to Britt Jones for early SM support plus the line, "surrender your bubble gum."

a dream once lost had its educational premiere at Metropolitan School of the Arts in 2023, directed by Matt Bassett and assistant directed by Ky Davis.

The cast included:
Naomi Aldrich (sophi)
Saniyya Rivera (attlea)
Mayumi Gant (counter-king, others)
Olivia Cooper (queen, aychpot, others)
Kara Molineux (emory, child, others)
Helena Marques (star, others)
Madison Schiffer (star, others)
Sunshine Smith (star, others)

Designed and supported by:
Heather Gifford (original vocal compositions)
Ky Davis (costumes)
Heather Mack (props)
Jennifer J. Hopkins (movement)
Mayumi Gant (sound)
Ky Davis (stage manager)

a note from the wizard. er, playwright.

Hello! I'm peeking out from behind the curtain to tell you that this piece is truly an offering for you. I invite your team to dare to be a bit vulnerable and quite imaginative together to make this your very own. You already have those tools! (Remember when you thought the floor was lava?)

I have had the honor of seeing this piece come to life in different iterations, including with a cast of 5 wonderful professional adult actors, and later with a cast of 8 wonderful middle/high school students. So I can say with certainty that this play offers some rare opportunities for theatremakers at every level of age and experience. And before we go any further young people can handle this. In fact, I believe that they deserve art like this. Actors as young as 13 have been part of the ensemble…we've had designers as young as 17… and audience members as young as elementary school-aged. Honestly, I think young people have even greater and more immediate access to this poetic language and playful world than we grownups do. With a bit of guidance and a lot of trust, they'll make this play better (more fun and more ache-y and more hopeful) than the one in my brain.

Okay, here are some thoughts/suggestions that might help as you read and imagine this play in your company's hands. This script is an impressionistic piece that plays like poetry, flowing into and out of images quickly, so the more nimble your production is, the better. Your actors' bodies and voices will be your best means of communicating place. Simple staging using interconnected limbs can give Sophi a tree to climb up or a hole to climb into. A sung Key of A can build to a chord that makes your Key Room fill the space. The stairway could be as simple as actors holding hands and forming a spiral that Sophi must follow. Casting is very flexible. With a cast of as few as five, the entire royal family can be represented. If you have access to a larger cast, you can have a sea of stars that watch Sophi throughout her journey, dipping in at different points to play a small role. Design is only as necessary as you find it. This play premiered in an art gallery in broad daylight as effectively as in a black box theater under stage lights. That said, in both of the productions mentioned, we found that a soundscape, either pre-recorded or created by actors singing/chanting/ humming at certain moments, did wonders.

Thank you, wherever you are out there, for considering this unconventional piece of theatre. I wrote this as a young ADHD adult who then grew up to have a kid on the Autism spectrum; unconventional art can mean an awful lot to us atypically-brained. And frankly…I think it speaks to the beautiful quirk-ster in all of us.

Be well, and happy *dream*-ing.

characters

sophi
attlea, *sophi's sister*

the stars, *a celestial chorus of 3 or more; their physicality helps to create each new location*
the queen, *sophi's mother*
emory, *sophi's brother*
a child
the oracle, *portrayed by live or pre-recorded music, or some other way entirely*
the counter-king
a turtle, *portrayed by actor, puppet, or some other way entirely*
a giant, *portrayed by actor(s), puppet, pre-recorded/offstage voice, or some other way entirely*
the association association
the monks
the twins
a voice
madam aychpot

note: the king, sophi's father, is spoken of but neither seen nor heard throughout the play. all of these roles, with the exception of the sisters--sophi and attlea—may be played by the actors portraying the stars.

*This printing is dedicated to Phil Perry,
the original Counter-King.*

"Everything lasts. It just moves, it just moves."

(At the play's open, the Stars chant either without words or in a language we do not understand as they take turns translating to the audience. During this sequence, the Queen solemnly walks across the stage, lost, and exits. Emory enters and begins to build a card castle. His right hand shakes.)

STAR 1
The time is a year descending.

STAR 2
The place, the Kingdom of Caras, far away from here yet very close.

STAR 3
A plague has enveloped the kingdom like a cloud, and the king himself has taken ill.

STAR 1
The royal House of Asra is in something of a dream state.

STAR 2
The entire kingdom waits as if suspended.

STAR 3
Suspended. A kingdom in a cloud. *(Emory's castle crumbles, and he exits. The Stars vanish. Sophi enters.)*

SOPHI
Father lies in bed all day. At first the plague made him fidgety; now it seems to paralyze him. His skin grows translucent, his sight becomes hazy. If you look closely at his chest, the heavy throbs of his heart become visible. I understand the people want to keep us safe. But there is something restless in me that will not be stilled. It moves as my mother does, *(Queen shuffles across again)* as my

SOPHI (CONT)
brother does *(Emory enters and begins with his cards again)*.
It moves with my father's feverish heart, and it pushes me
out into the world. I have heard of an oracle. I have heard
that if you follow the stars for half a night, you will come to
an oracle. *(The Stars appear and begin to chant. Sophi
follows them to the steps of the Oracle.)*

the steps

(Sophi enters, humming the Stars' chant.)

CHILD
(Sitting on the steps of the Oracle) Surrender your hand!

SOPHI
...

CHILD
What?

SOPHI
Nothing. That makes me think of a poem I heard. "Surrender
your--"

CHILD
Hand?

SOPHI
No.

CHILD
Hat?

SOPHI
No.

                    CHILD

Billy goat.

                    SOPHI

No. --what?

                    CHILD

Bubble gum!

                    SOPHI

Bubble gum! "Surrender your bubble gum." Yay.

                    CHILD

I like it.

                    SOPHI

Me, too. That's what I told him.

                    CHILD

Who?

                    SOPHI

Him. The boy who told me the poem. It was his. I told him I
liked it. I don't think he believed me.

                    CHILD

...hey!

                    SOPHI

What?

                    CHILD

Your hand!

                    SOPHI

O, yes. Sorry. Here.

CHILD

Circle, circle, dot, dot--

SOPHI

Are you kidding me? All this was for a cootie shot?

CHILD

What's a cootie shot?

SOPHI

...

CHILD

This is your ticket in to the Oracle.

SOPHI

(A beat. She finally turns to enter the chamber.)

the oracle

ORACLE

(violin zings)

SOPHI

Yes, I'm here about--

ORACLE

(violin zings)

SOPHI

Yes, I've had my...cootie shot--

ORACLE

(violin zings)

SOPHI

Is this a joke?

ORACLE

(violin zings)

SOPHI

I'm sorry, it's just--

ORACLE

(zing)

SOPHI

I'm a little--

ORACLE

(zing)

SOPHI

Teapot? No!

ORACLE

(violin zings)

SOPHI

I'm sorry. I should laugh, I just didn't expect you to
be...funny. I imagine oracles have kind of a bad rap since
Oedipus.

ORACLE

(laugh-like zings)

SOPHI

Thanks. So, Mr.--

ORACLE

(zing!)

SOPHI

Miss Oracle...I need...help.

ORACLE

(Song of Instruction)

SOPHI

Oh.   oh. *(Exits chamber.)*

the steps

CHILD

She's good, isn't she?

SOPHI

Well, I won't know until I know, now will I? *(Oracle zings laughter from within.)*

CHILD

Here, I drew this for you. It's your map.

SOPHI

But it only takes me part of the way.

CHILD

I know. After that you're off the map. That's the good stuff.

the start

> *(Sophi stands alone for a beat, paralyzed. Attlea enters.)*

ATTLEA

(To audience) Instructions on Beginning a Journey.

ATTLEA & SOPHI

How do you begin a journey?

STARS

With a single-- *(Stars and Attlea stomp with Sophi's first step. All exit except Sophi.)*

SOPHI

(Almost surprised by her first step. A beat before she takes another.) Okay. Okay. This isn't so bad. How is it that once you have purpose it feels as though you must learn to walk all over again?

ATTLEA

(re-entering) Good question, sis.

SOPHI

(To audience) I've been seeing Attlea lately. Sometimes she just hangs around me quietly, and sometimes we have entire conversations. I don't know if she's visiting me or I'm making her up, but I see her nonetheless.

ATTLEA

Where are you going?

SOPHI

Over the river and through the woods.

ATTLEA

Smart aleck.

SOPHI

No, seriously. I'm supposed to cross the rivulets and the Blink Forest to get to a key room in the Tumble Hills.

ATTLEA

Hunh. How will you cross the rivulets?

SOPHI

I don't know. I think they're small. I think you can just hop over them. *(They appear. She does. A single tree appears.)* So here's the Blink-- *(the tree disappears)* Forest...

ATTLEA

Blink and you'll miss it!

SOPHI

I guess so. This is why I don't take walks, Attlea. They're just a painful reminder of what a tiny, tiny kingdom we live in.

ATTLEA

All the world is here, Sophi.

SOPHI

(grunts. A beat. The Stars appear and ball up into hills. To the hills:) So, one of you holds a key.

HILL 1	HILL 2	HILL 3
Key!		
	Key!	
		Key!

SOPHI

Hunh.

ATTLEA

Hey Sophi, remember what we use to play in the backyard? I think we should play that now.

SOPHI

O ghost of my sister, did you bring horseshoes?

ATTLEA

No, not that. The other game. ...ribbit...

HILL 1	HILL 2	HILL 3

Ribbit!

              Ribbit!

                              Ribbit!

SOPHI
Leapfrog? *(Attlea nods.)* Attlea, I've got journeying to do.

ATTLEA
Come on! *(Begins to leap over the hills, one at a time.)*

SOPHI
This is ridiculous. *(But she joins. Each time she leaps over a hill, a tone is sounded. When the sisters have bounded over each hill, the hills become stars again.)*

the key room

(The sisters look around in awe)

ATTLEA
So which key is the one you need?

SOPHI
I don't know. I don't know. The Oracle just said to get the key from the key room. *The* key. Which made me think there'd be just one key, not shelves of them.

ATTLEA
They have writing on them.

SOPHI
(Reads) "Key of A--" *(Stars hold a note in the key of A)* "Key of C--" *(same)*

ATTLEA
"Key of G--" *(same)*

SOPHI

"Key of D--" *(same)*

ATTLEA

"Key of Q--" *(Silence. Attlea and Sophi look at each other. Exit with the key.)*

the end of the map

SOPHI

That was-- *(Realizes she is alone).* Oh. Okay. Bye, Attlea. *(Some time passes, quietly.)*

STAR 1

Sophi continued her journey--

STAR 2

carrying the Key of Q and the weight of questions--

STAR 3

until she came to--

STARS

The End of the Map.

SOPHI

(Stops. Looks around.) I'm nowhere.

STAR 1

(A beat.) She began to think:

SOPHI

I don't know what I'm doing.

STAR 2

And:

SOPHI

The instructions said all roads would lead me...

STAR 3

And:

SOPHI

Maybe I made them up. The instructions. Maybe I just
thought I heard them in her song...maybe I've made all of
this up. Like I made Attlea's ghost up.

ATTLEA

(walking by) Maybe you made yourself up. *(Exits.)*

SOPHI

(A beat) She's very snarky, this ghost. *(Silence for a time.
Then:)*

STAR 1

An inbetween space at an inbetween hour, thinking:

SOPHI

I miss my father. *(The Stars appear to Sophi.)* There are stars
here, at least. It's hard to see them over the palace
sometimes. But here, where there is nothing--well, Nowhere
is lit by stars. *(To the Stars.)* You brought me to the Oracle. I
wish you could show me the way now...*(The Stars point.
Sophi, unbelieving for a beat, finally obeys. A child appears
before her.)*

the guest book

CHILD
Greetings. What is your name?

SOPHI
Sophi.

CHILD
(flipping through) O, no, you're already in here. Like, a lot.
You don't need to sign in.

SOPHI
But I've never been here.

CHILD
That doesn't matter. You're in the book.

SOPHI
Are you sure it's me? Maybe it's another Sophi.

CHILD
Another Sophi with a slug-shaped scar on her right elbow
from when a boy who blocked out the sun ran her over?

SOPHI
...

CHILD
(smiles)

SOPHI
How did you--is that written there?

CHILD
No. But I can tell by the handwriting.

SOPHI

Geez-oh-Petes.

CHILD

You got that saying from your best friend, Dorene. She's studying law in another kingdom now. *(Sophi stumbles away from the child, flabbergasted. The child calls:)* Welcome to the Repository!

the counter-king

COUNTER-KING

(Building a house of cards. At Sophi's approach:) It is you, it is you! I was told about you, I was told you were coming. O, hooray!

SOPHI

What are you building?

COUNTER-KING

A castle of cards. The House of Asra, to be precise.

SOPHI

This is familiar....

COUNTER-KING

O, much that is here will be familiar. And much as well will be surprising.

SOPHI

Hunh. Are you the king of this place?

COUNTER-KING

Of the Repository. Yes, yes. Which runs counter to the un-Repository at times— O, silly mortals!--and thusly I am called Counter-King. You may ask me things, and I will point you places.

SOPHI

I'm here to save my father. I was told I'd find what I need here.

COUNTER-KING

You will.

SOPHI

...Where?

COUNTER-KING

Eachwhere.

SOPHI

Eachwhere?

COUNTER-KING

Eachwhere, eachwhere. Each-and-everywhere.

SOPHI

Can you tell me what it *is* that I need?

COUNTER-KING

Many things. Firstly, this. *(Hands her a box.)*

SOPHI

What is this for?

COUNTER-KING

For the things you must gather. We hate to see them go, but I suppose they never should have been here in the first place, sooo, Mazel Tov, young star- gazer.

SOPHI

...

COUNTER-KING

(points to them) There are stars gazing at you.

SOPHI

But, I don't, I--

COUNTER-KING

Darling, I'd love to chat further--O, glorious speech!--but I must push you along. You've got a lot to do, and you're needed elsewhere. But I will be here, should you come by again!

SOPHI

Which way should I go?

COUNTER-KING

That way! *(He points nowhere.)*

SOPHI

(A beat. She chooses a direction and begins walking. She comes to a tree with a treehouse in it.) Hunh. *(She moves toward the tree; stops.)*

STAR 1

Before climbing the tree, Sophi is compelled to look closer.

STAR 2

She notices something tiny, descending just above her.

STARS

She holds out her hand.

STAR 3

Her eyes adjust and she notices they are all around her.

SOPHI

Inchworms!

STAR 1

Something stirs within the caverns of her memory.

STAR 2

Not a remembrance of her own, but a connection to one.

STARS

The inchworms

STAR 3

disappear. *(Sophi climbs the tree.)*

the treehouse

(There are various objects in the treehouse--a telescope; maybe a stack of books, binoculars, a magic lantern, jars of shells and rocks and other childhood treasures from the outside world. Sophi spends some time with the items before speaking.)

SOPHI

(Looking out a window) The view is incredible. *(Using the telescope)* Look at those stars! *(The stars wave to her. She opens a book.)* "The sand eel is not an eel but like an eel." *(She smiles)* Silly slithery. *(Grabs a shell)* Wow. Look at this thing. *Water* made this thing. Water and sand and time. So

SOPHI (CONT)

many miracles...

ATTLEA

...taken for granted. *(To Sophi, above her:)* O sister, my sister, let down your hair!

SOPHI

I'm coming, I'm coming. *(Puts the shell in her box. Climbs down.)* Hey, where were you earlier?

ATTLEA

Nowhere.

SOPHI

Well, I was nowhere, too, and I certainly didn't see you.

ATTLEA

Aww, were you lonely?

SOPHI

No. *(A beat)* Hey, Attlea, what is this called? I can't remember. *(Shows her the shell)*

ATTLEA

That's a shell.

SOPHI

A shell! I can't believe I forgot that!

ATTLEA

Maybe you're tired.

SOPHI

Maybe. *(They approach the Counter-King)* Hi...what are you doing here? I left you that way. *(Points)*

COUNTER-KING
It is you, it is you! I was told about you, I was told you were coming. O, hooray!

SOPHI
...but we just met a few minutes ago.

COUNTER-KING
Pardon?

SOPHI
You don't remember me?

COUNTER-KING
Remember? I barely exist! *(Laughs)* O, what a fantastic little box. What's in it? May I see?

SOPHI
You gave it to me.

COUNTER-KING
O, I wouldn't put it by me. I have excellent taste. Open?

SOPHI
(Opens the box) Just a shell so far.

COUNTER-KING
What shell? What's a shell? This is wonder!

SOPHI
Wonder?

COUNTER-KING
It's wonder, it's wonder--O, marvelous wonder! Keep it. Keep it as long as you can.

SOPHI

But how is it possible--

COUNTER-KING

Possible, possible. Ah, that reminds me. I'm to tell you a
thing. *(leans in)* There is a way to get from Possibility to
Actuality: You wake up. *(winks)*

SOPHI

(a beat) You really don't remember me?

COUNTER-KING

What? O, I'm not the same. Not the same "I" that Was just
however ago. Change changes things.

SOPHI

Where am I? *(Counter-King disappears. The Stars chant.)*

STARS

On Your Way.

SOPHI

But where exactly am I?

ATTLEA

The sign says "Italy."

italy

SOPHI

What? I don't understand. We can't be in Italy. There's a
whole body of water between us and Italy that we didn't
cross. Maybe it's a city named Italy that we've just never
heard of.

ATTLEA

No, it's the country.

SOPHI

How do you know?

ATTLEA

It's right here on the sign. It says, "Italy: The Country."

SOPHI

(Continues walking silently. After a few beats:) How's
Emory?

ATTLEA

The same.

SOPHI

(A beat) Why do you think we're in Italy?

ATTLEA

I'm not anywhere. You're in Italy.

SOPHI

Fine. Whatever. I just don't understand what I'm doing here.
I know I was sent here. I just--

ATTLEA

"There was the dream of you, and there is you."

SOPHI

What?

ATTLEA

What?

SOPHI

What did you just say? About a dream?

ATTLEA

I didn't say anything.

SOPHI

But I heard you--

ATTLEA

Heard me what?

TURTLE

Heard me what?

SOPHI & ATTLEA
(Fall quiet. Look around.)

TURTLE
Down. *(They look down.)* Hello.

SOPHI
Attlea, did the turtle just speak?

TURTLE
You may address me directly. But yes, I did indeed just speak.

SOPHI
...so the turtles in Italy speak?

TURTLE
This is not *actual* Italy. It is a *perceived* Italy. All part of the Repository.

SOPHI
...does Italy even have turtles?

TURTLE
Doesn't matter. This *perception* does.

SOPHI
So why aren't you *perceptively* speaking Italian?

TURTLE
I am. You just happen to understand it.

SOPHI
(Buries her face in her hands)

TURTLE
Calm yourself, child. You have been sent to me. I will help you defeat the giant. I must sacrifice myself to a soup you shall make--

SOPHI
O my god!

TURTLE
Heh. Heh. Just kidding. That's one of my favorite tickles. Heh. No no, look now, together we will defeat the giant.

SOPHI
Giant? What giant?

TURTLE
The giant that has stepped on the gumption that you need.

SOPHI
But I've got gumption. Arguably too much.

TURTLE
(The ground shakes) No time to explain! He comes, he comes! Quickly, you must devise a plan! We must get him to lie down.

SOPHI
(To the giant) ...I love you!

TURTLE & GIANT
What?

ATTLEA
Ha!

SOPHI
I am a poet, and I am in love with you. It came upon me just now, as my heart shuddered with your gallantly thunderous step.

TURTLE
This tactic is questionable.

GIANT
I'm sorry, I have a girlfriend.

SOPHI
Please may I just compose a sonnet for you?

GIANT
...o.k.

SOPHI
O, thank you! Thank you. Now, to do this, I must get a good look at your eyes. For the eyes are the window to the soul, and your soul is the doorway through which I will emerge a better person, and a more inspired poet.

GIANT
...o.k. I could pick you up--

SOPHI

No, please, I am afraid of heights. But if you come down to my level, I shall be able to get a good look.

GIANT

My knees are bad--crouching is very difficult for my kind.

SOPHI

So I've read.

TURTLE

(To Attlea) Did she really know that?

ATTLEA

I wouldn't put it past her.

SOPHI

Perhaps you could lie down? A brief bend of the knees, but then you'd be stretched out, and you could relax for a while as I gazed into the--

TURTLE

Gooey orbs--

SOPHI

Gooey orbs *(To the TURTLE?!)* of your eyes.

GIANT

...o.k. *(He begins to lie down.)*

SOPHI

(To the Turtle) What now?

TURTLE

His shoes! Make a beeline for his shoes! The gumption will be stuck to the bottom of one of them.

ATTLEA

Eww. *(They run to his shoes.)*

SOPHI

(Spots the gumption and goes for it) Ugh, it's sticky!

TURTLE

It's gumption! *(He helps her; they finally fall back with the gumption.)*

GIANT

(Lying on the ground) Here they are! Here are my eyes! ...hey, where'd you go?

ATTLEA

Way to give him the lie, sis.

TURTLE

I'm afraid you'll have to pun on the run. Italy closes in 3 minutes.

SOPHI

Are you joking? But what do I do with the gumption?

TURTLE

Keep it. Guard it. Exit where you entered and enjoy the show!

SOPHI

Show? *(Attlea pulls Sophi. They briskly exit as:)*

STARS

(Appear in a line and sing a childish Italian song with cuckoo-clock movements. They hold a sign proclaiming, "You are now leaving Italy. Ciao-ciao!")

SOPHI

(Laughing, catching her breath) Ha, wow, it's- *(Realizes she's alone)* Attlea? Why do you always leave when I want you here? *(Puts the gumption into the box)* Gumption and Wonder. Or, gum and a shell, to the undiscerning eye. *(Closes the box)* I have the gumption to wonder how these little things can cure a body, a heart, my father. *(As she walks, she hears faint vocals that lead her to a cave.)*

the cave

> *(Sophi enters the cave, follows the growing, echoing sounds of a chanted Latin Mass, sung by the Stars with hymnals. She approaches them, and is given a hymnal. She flips through it.)*

SOPHI

The pages are all blank. What are you saying?

STARS

(Continue to chant)

SOPHI

I don't understand what you're saying.

STARS

(Continue to chant; point to something downstage left.)

SOPHI

(Goes to the object. It is a stone tablet. She reads:) "I am the Light, the Truth and the Way." *(She lifts the tablet to reveal a hole in the ground. She climbs down into it; re- enters upstage center, into a different scene. The stage is empty, bathed in blue. There is the sound of water dancing with a shore.)*

ATTLEA

(Walking by) You should open the book.

SOPHI

It's blank.

ATTLEA

Open it again.

SOPHI

(Opens the book) How did you do that?

ATTLEA

I didn't do it, I just knew about it.

SOPHI

Attlea, this is Dad's handwriting.

ATTLEA

I know. And he's looking for it. *(Exits)*

SOPHI

(Reading from the book:) "Instructions for walking across water: Be prepared to swim." *(Smiles)* That's good advice, Dad. *(She steps onto the water)*

the church

(Sophi crosses the water and comes to a church with no roof.)

STAR 1

The church with no roof is where Father first learnt of the sky.

STAR 2

It had been there before, of course. It had always been there.

STAR 3

He just never noticed it. Not until he passed into the church *(Sophi walks in)* -

STAR 1

touched its stone walls, moving his fingertips over years, centuries, even, and memories *(Sophi does this)* -

STAR 2

and finally, cautiously, afraid of the something in him that knew it would be overwhelmed-

STAR 3 & ATTLEA

he looked up. *(Sophi looks up.)*

SOPHI

(A beat) The sky. *(A bit of sky floats down to her. She places it in the box and wanders out of the church.)*

ATTLEA

Outside it is green, and dewy.

SOPHI

Do we?

ATTLEA

Dewy.

SOPHI

Do we what?

ATTLEA

Dewy leaves.

SOPHI

Do we leave?

ATTLEA

...

SOPHI

...

ATTLEA

(to audience) We never could understand each other.

SOPHI

Attlea, what are you doing here?

ATTLEA

The church.

SOPHI

Yes. Thank you. Yes. I see. Now go away.

ATTLEA

You've been here before.

SOPHI

What? I don't want you here.

ATTLEA

You've always been here before.

SOPHI

You're dead!

ATTLEA

I'm telling you. I'm telling you. There was the dream of you....

ASSOCIATION
(the Stars, in bowties) Hello.

SOPHI & ATTLEA
Hello. *(A beat. Two beats. Three b--)*

ASSOC. 1
Do it!

ASSOC. 2
(to 1) Marley!

ASSOC. 3
(to 1 & 2) We can wait.

ASSOC. 1
(to SOPHI & Attlea) Say a word!

ASSOC. 2
(to SOPHI & Attlea) We're sorry. He's new.

ASSOC. 3
They're always jumpy when they're new.

SOPHI
It's o.k. What word should we say?

ASSOC. 2
O, any old word.

ASSOC. 3
Any new word, too.

ATTLEA
Polliwog.

ASSOC. 1

Polliwog leads to--

ASSOC. 2

Furry leads to--

ASSOC. 3

Fireplace.

ASSOC. 1
(to 2 & 3) Can I be on the end next time?

SOPHI

What just happened?

ASSOC. 3

Forgive our manners. We are--

ASSOC. 1

The Association Association!

ASSOC. 2

Making associations that no one else would make.

ATTLEA

Hurricane.

ASSOC. 3

Hurricane leads to--

ASSOC. 2

Helicopter leads to--

ASSOC. 1

Hamburger sign! *(to 2 & 3)* That was a good one. *(They nod amongst themselves, pleased.)*

                    ATTLEA

Clouds!

                    ASSOC. 1

Clouds lead to--

                    ASSOC. 3

Bunnies lead to--

                    ASSOC. 2

Sophi.

                    SOPHI

That's me. *(They nod)* ...Attlea.

                    ASSOC. 1

Attlea leads to--

                    ASSOC. 2

Pendant leads to--

                    ASSOC. 3

Tall grass.

                    SOPHI

(to Attlea) You had a pendant.

                    ATTLEA

A big one. I got it as a present and it was too heavy for my
chain. It fell off--

                    SOPHI

In the meadow--

                    ATTLEA

I cried and Dad tried to find it--

SOPHI

But the grass was too tall. *(They turn on the Association members, who have disappeared into the Stars.)* Nothing here lasts! *(Attlea disappears. The Counter-King appears in her stead.)*

COUNTER-KING

Quite the opposite. *Everything* lasts. It just moves, it just moves.

SOPHI

You. Do you know me now?

COUNTER-KING

O, I've known you all your life.

SOPHI

All my life? I don't even know what that means.

COUNTER-KING

"Life." A simple game of gestures and words. An interplay of breath, thought and emotion. Real action occasionally involved. The use of energy, the constant use of energy. Adding and subtracting. Finally tipping over.

SOPHI

Well, what do I do about it?

COUNTER-KING

About it? With. No, with. Make a chain. Of daisies, of paper. Dangle it above you and behind you. Ha! It'll be fun.

SOPHI

Will it?

COUNTER-KING

O, yes. Yes beyond yes. It...will...be...fun.

SOPHI

(a beat) My father is dying.

COUNTER-KING

Madam Aychpot knows about dying. She's been doing it for ages.

SOPHI

Madam Aychpot? Who is she?

COUNTER-KING

O, an old resident of the Repository. She lives alone in an inn, and chooses a different room for every season: Winter, Spring, Summer, Floating and Fall.

SOPHI

Floating?

COUNTER-KING

O, yes, Floating. Floating is the season that was created on the day God rested. He sighed, and out it came. It really only lasts a day. It is the season of turning and lightness. Air is cooled and Fall is nigh. It is because of this brief season that poetry exists. Every year during Floating, Madam Aychpot retires to the water- colored room and types a single word.

SOPHI

This is familiar....

COUNTER-KING

O, much that is here will be familiar.

SOPHI

And much as well will be surprising.

COUNTER-KING

Yes, yes! Good guess!

SOPHI

I'm in a nightmare, aren't I?

COUNTER-KING

No, not you. *He* is, but not yet you.

SOPHI

He? Who is he?

COUNTER-KING

I must go. Seeds to sow. Keep collecting! He's expecting!
(exits)

> *(Sophi walks. The Stars appear; they hum or chant the "Song of Instruction." They stop short when Sophi comes to a canyon.)*

the canyon

SOPHI

(sitting on the edge) I have come to the edge of the world.

ATTLEA

Yeah.

SOPHI

...I didn't know the world had one.

ATTLEA

It doesn't.

SOPHI

O. *(A beat)* Does this mean I've failed.

ATTLEA

Of course not.

SOPHI

Do you miss me, Attlea?

ATTLEA

You're right here.

SOPHI

Yeah, but...you know. It's not like we can really be together.
Not like we used to.

ATTLEA

Yeah. I know. I guess I miss you the way you miss yourself.

SOPHI

I miss you, too.

ATTLEA

I know, Sophi. It's o.k. I know. Now, what are you going to
do about this canyon? *(A beat. Sophi jumps in. The Stars
emit a dying fall. Attlea smiles.)*

the monks

> *(A monastery. Tibetan monks silently work to
> create a mandala on the floor. They are almost
> done. Sophi enters.)*

SOPHI

There was the dream of you...

MONKS

And there is you. *(They finish the mandala. A beat. They
blow it away.)*

SOPHI

Why-? *(One of the monks gives her a handful of the colored sand. She places it in her box.)*

MONK 1

Earth.

SOPHI

(Looking at the sand) Earth. *(A beat)* How much more do I need? *(Monk 1 stands. Monk 2 stands. Monk 3 stands.)* Three. Three things. *(They bow to her and exit. She sighs. A beat. Finally, she begins to hum the "Song of Instruction" and walks on.)*

the museum

SOPHI

(Reading a placard) "The Museum of Mediocre Mischief."

ATTLEA

(Enters) You still don't know where you are, do you?

SOPHI

I'm in a museum.

ATTLEA

Read the finer print.

SOPHI

"Bad jokes, gags and mundane magic from the collection of King Hal of Asra." ...so?

ATTLEA

Sophi, that's Dad.

                            SOPHI
Dad? ...Dad! O god, Sophi, why do I keep forgetting?

                            ATTLEA
Attlea. And it's only natural--this place is overpowering.

                            SOPHI
This place--you know what it is. *(Attlea nods)* What?

                            ATTLEA
A museum.

                            SOPHI
No, this whole place. What is it?

                            ATTLEA
The Repository.

                            SOPHI
But what does that *mean*?

                            ATTLEA
It means it's a warehouse. A series of caverns. You've been
here before, you know.

                            SOPHI
What?

                            ATTLEA
You've always been here before.

                            SOPHI
I've never been here before.

                            ATTLEA
You were born here, and you live here.

SOPHI
O, what do you know? You're dead.

ATTLEA
I'm telling you. I'm telling you.

SOPHI
Dead dead dead! Please respect your station in life. You cannot be real. You cannot be real. I WEPT FOR YOU. *(The Stars indistinctly echo this last line. Sophi is alone. A beat. She looks around.)* The Museum of Mediocre Mischief. *(She begins to toy with the museum's contents, which include Practical Jokes as well as Impractical ones. There is an unmarked tin can. She opens it. The Stars begin to chuckle but abruptly stop when she replaces the lid. This happens a few times. Sophi regards the can before placing it in her box.)* Gumption. Wonder. Earth and Sky. And Laughter.

STARS
(to audience only) How to Make a Father. *(a beat)*

STAR 1
She closes the box--

STAR 2
Smiles, thoughtful--

STAR 3
And passes through the museum.

SOPHI
Two things left. Two things left.

TWIN 1
(Offstage. Takes up the phrase as a chant.) Two things left. Two things left! Two things left!

SOPHI

*(Approaches a set of twins, each planted in front of a door.
One is fast asleep.)* Do you know what things?

TWIN 1

(same chant) What things left! What things left!

SOPHI

So that's a "no."

TWIN 1

No things left! No things left!

SOPHI

...

TWIN 1

You look grumpy.

SOPHI

I am grumpy.

TWIN 1

Grumpies should see Dr. SiR.

SOPHI

Doc—There's a doctor here?

TWIN 1

Mm-hmm!

SOPHI

Why didn't anyone tell me? *(Twin 1 shrugs.)* Where?
Where's Dr. SiR? My father is sick-- where's Dr. SiR?

TWIN 1

He's past here, butcha can't pass here until you pass here

(indicates door he is guarding).

SOPHI
Please, can I pass here?

TWIN 1
Into Possibility?

SOPHI
I don't know--is that what this is?

TWIN 1
Mm-hmm!

SOPHI
Then yes, yes.

TWIN 1
Only if you have the key.

SOPHI
Well, what about that door? *(points to the other)*

TWIN 1
Uh-uh, no way, that's Actuality and it doesn't even have a
lock. That's my brother in front of it and he always sleeps.
He doesn't have to stay awake--who wants to visit Actuality?
And anyway, even if they wanted to, how ever would they
get in?

SOPHI
Okay, all right, where do I get the key?

ATTLEA
You've got the key.

SOPHI

(Turning on her) Didn't I-- *(fishes out the Key of Q)* You're right. The Key of Q. *(shows it to Twin 1)* Is this it?

TWIN 1

I don't know.

SOPHI

But you guard the door!

TWIN 1

(chants again) Guard the door! Guard the door! That's what silly twins are for!

SOPHI

(To Attlea) I'm going to punch him. *(Attlea takes the key)*

ATTLEA

(to Twin 1) May I?

TWIN 1

Mm-hmm! *(She tries the key. It works; the door swings open. Twin 1 cheers. Sophi and Attlea enter.)*

possibility

(The room is bare, but somehow twinkling, somehow alive. Out of habit, the sisters look first for answers, then begin to enjoy this new question.)

SOPHI

It's so nice in here...so warm and full. I think I'll live here.

ATTLEA

Sophi--

SOPHI

No, no, it's perfect. It's perfect. I feel so light. Where did all the weight go?

ATTLEA

It's still there, Sophi. You just don't see it right now.

SOPHI

This is everything. This is the dream of me. It's like being in a star--all this light. Just weightless light. *(to herself)* Please can I keep this?

ATTLEA

You need to fill the box.

SOPHI

The box! *(she opens it)*

ATTLEA

(searching the room) Hunh. There aren't any objects here. *(One of the Stars appears to her)*

STAR

Pick a hand. *(Attlea chooses. She is given a thing with feathers. The star disappears.)*

SOPHI

(turning to Attlea) What is the thing with feathers?

ATTLEA

Hope. *(she puts it in the box)*

SOPHI

I am there. I have everything I wanted.

ATTLEA

No, you don't. What about Father?

SOPHI

What's a father?

ATTLEA

Sophi, these things are not for you to keep.

SOPHI

What?

ATTLEA

You must blow them away.

SOPHI

What are you talking about? What is your name?

ATTLEA

Remember the monks.

SOPHI

Monks—

ATTLEA

Remember the stars.

SOPHI

Stars--

ATTLEA

And the Oracle. What did the Oracle say?

SOPHI

There was an Oracle. She told me to go.

ATTLEA

And?

SOPHI
And…and which way to go. In a song.

ATTLEA
And what else?

SOPHI
(a beat) She told me Madam Aychpot's word. She told me the one word for this year.

ATTLEA
Did she tell you how to get into Actuality?

SOPHI
No.

ATTLEA
Are you sure?

SOPHI
Yes. Why?

ATTLEA
You have to get in there. She didn't tell you...

SOPHI
Actuality…wake--

ATTLEA
What?

SOPHI
Wake up, "you wake up!" The Counter-King told me.

ATTLEA
But you're awake.

SOPHI

Am I?

ATTLEA

Yes. You wake up...you wake up...you--

TWIN 1

(from outside the door. Cannot help himself. Begins to chant)
--wake up! You wake up!

ATTLEA & TWIN 1

You wake up! You wake up! *(Attlea motions for Sophi to join)*

ATTLEA, SOPHI & TWIN 1

You wake--

TWIN 2

(waking) Hey, hey! What's the big idea?

TWIN 1

O, no! *(the room changes. A disembodied voice is heard overhead.)*

VOICE

Welcome to Actuality.

actuality

(There is a window in this room. It faces the audience. Sophi and Attlea make their way to it.)

ATTLEA

(points out the window) Sophi, look. *(Sophi joins her sister. Through the window, they watch Mother make her way across the stage in an echo of the opening sequence; Emory*

sits alone and builds a house of cards. On either side of the window, there is an atmosphere of waiting and sterility, as in a hospital corridor. Some moments pass and then there is a rumble, a tremor. Everyone feels it. Mother stops; Emory's castle has crumbled; the Counter-King appears in the middle of the scene, below the window, and addresses Sophi soberly. The lights have gone out and the Stars take over to create the only light.)

COUNTER-KING

Sophi, there is not much time. Your father-

SOPHI

Wha--

COUNTER-KING

You must hurry. The last object is in the Floating room, then you can exit the Repository.

SOPHI

But how will these things help him? Why can't I just go now?

COUNTER-KING

These things are his, Sophi. They are things he fears he has lost. But he has not lost them, he has only forgotten. The plague makes him long for who he was. To counter the plague, you must show him that all of these pieces are still here, they are still a part of him. They never left and they never will. He is all of these moments together--a string of moments *(the Stars echo this line)*--not just this one now. Give him these bits of himself and you give him his story. You give him his weight in the world. *(Another tremor)* Quickly, Sophi. You must go!

SOPHI

(yells) But where am I? *(Another tremor. Lights out.)*

VOICE
(in darkness) Paging Dr. SiR. Paging Dr. SiR.

madam aychpot

*(Madam Aychpot sits alone in a dark room.
Sophi approaches, but is compelled to keep a
certain distance. They are quiet for a moment.)*

SOPHI
(finally) Your room is so dark.

MADAM
It's Winter.

SOPHI
(a beat) It is said that you are always dying.

MADAM
Who said that? C.K.?

SOPHI
C.K.- the Counter-King, yes.

MADAM
So like him. He's so dramatic.

SOPHI
Is it not true, then?

MADAM
I've lived far too much to ever be dying. I'm on a
"denouement" – that, I'll concede – but I'm not dying.

SOPHI

My father-

MADAM

is dying. Mm.

SOPHI

How do you know?

MADAM

It's my business to know. How do *you* know?

SOPHI

It's my business to save him.

MADAM

From what? Death? Good luck with that.

SOPHI

From untimely death.

MADAM

What death is timely?

SOPHI

Alright, then from sadness.

MADAM

Mm. Sadness is necessary.

SOPHI

Alright, then from lightness.

MADAM

Now you're talkin'. My favorite season is one of lightness,
but you can't live in it. No way. That room is good for only
one day.

SOPHI

Are you rhyming?

MADAM

Have you only now realized?

SOPHI

You've only now begun.

MADAM

You're clever.

SOPHI

I'm desperate.

MADAM.

Mm. You have my word. You don't need me.

SOPHI

(moves to exit. Stops and turns back to her.) Are you
someone my father loved?

MADAM

(smiles) It's funny that you don't recognize me. Although it
also makes sense. We know each other in such a specific and
fragile way. *(a beat.)* The Counter-King must have his
queen. Take care, Sophi. But don't worry about taking care
of us. You're saving *you*. That's what you're supposed to do.
*(Sophi passes slowly through the room, as if lost for a
moment.)*

dr. sir

*(Sophi is alone in another room. There is a
screen onto which are projected an assortment*

of dream images. Perhaps they are slides;
perhaps they are moving images like old home
videos. Whatever they are, they are constantly
changing.)

SOPHI

I've dreamed this before. Magenta, with an airship. *(She*
moves closer to the screen, and makes out a logo on the
bottom of it.) "The Dream-Room Screen-Room." Dr. SiR. *(A*
beat.) I know where I am, Dad. These are your dreams, and I
know where I am. Your stories, your travels...you always
said you won Mom's heart with ridiculous jokes. You
watched the monks for hours; you slept in the treehouse all
the time. You used to make up stories about a giant and a
turtle when Attlea and I couldn't sleep. I can't believe it.
This is you. *(She watches for a few more moments. Then*
there is a rumble.) I have to go.

floating

(A bit of adventure storytelling briskly told in
minimum light. Perhaps Sophi acts out the
narration, with the help of sound effects.)

STAR 1

Sophi passes through the doorway into the Floating room

STAR 2

stepping onto a platform that seems to be floating itself.

STAR 3

There is a welcome mat and then a drop-off

STAR 1

into water

STAR 2

a lake

STAR 3

where a floor should be.

STAR 1

Ahead she sees a boat

STAR 2

a canoe

STAR 3

she reaches out

STAR 1

and pulls it to her

STAR 2

she climbs in

STAR 3

picks up the paddle

STAR 1

but suddenly what was placid has come to life

STAR 2

there are ripples, then waves

STAR 3

tiny but growing

STAR 1

then a rumble

STAR 2

the entire room shakes

STAR 3

bits of ceiling fall like snow

STAR 1

she cuts fiercely through the water

STAR 2

it splashes over the sides of the boat

STAR 3

the water crashes

STARS

the boat tips!

STAR 1

but Sophi remembers her father's instructions. *(a beat)*

STARS

She walks.

STAR 1

She reaches the other side

STAR 2

the other shore

`STAR 3

similar to the first but with a desk

STAR 1

and a typewriter.

STAR 2

She knows what she must do.

STAR 3

She sits at the desk

STAR 1

and types a single word.

STAR 2

The water calms.

STAR 3

The world settles. *(Everyone freezes. Attlea walks onstage, in front of the scene. Addresses the audience)*

ATTLEA

And poetry was given back to Father. The final ingredient. *(Lights out.)*

again

(There is the sound of water dancing with a shore. There is the sound of a chanted Latin Mass. There is the sound of the Oracle zinging. The lights come up.)

ATTLEA

(Still to audience, as Sophi walks in but does not see her.) This is the room they call "Again." It must happen. It must happen. *(The Stars enter as the Association Association.)*

ASSOC. 1

Do it, do it! Give us a word!

ASSOC.. 2 & 3

(to 1) Marley!

COUNTER-KING

(voice only) It is you, it is you!

ASSOC. 1

You leads to--

ASSOC. 2

home leads to--

ASSOC. 3

staaaairrwaaaay. *(They begin to laugh a la the Museum of Mediocre Mischief. The various sounds of the Repository create a cacophony that Sophi rushes through to get to the next empty room.)*

breadcrumbs

(Part of the "Song of Instruction" is heard as Sophi recalls--)

SOPHI

She said my memories will lead me back. But I have forgotten how to remember.

ATTLEA

(to audience) "Remember." Verb. To re-member. Re-number. Call upon and categorize. Pull apart to put together. Re-member.

SOPHI

Where do I begin, Attlea?

ATTLEA

Pick a word. Any old word, or any new word, too.

SOPHI

Inchworms.

ATTLEA

His.

SOPHI

Giant.

ATTLEA

His.

SOPHI

Water.

ATTLEA

Qualify.

SOPHI

Ocean.

ATTLEA

His.

SOPHI

Puddle.

ATTLEA

Ah! Yours. *(Attlea kisses her sister on the cheek and exits.)*

SOPHI

A puddle in a dip in the sidewalk. I am standing like a tree, watching a tree. Leaves and branches perfectly reflected. And for extended moments, the puddle does not move. The

SOPHI (CONT)

water is a film over a glass container, holding a treetop. *(A beat, then a tiny noise is heard offstage.)* A noise so small in a world of quiet- it was a ladybug. It has fallen through a crack in the window of a white white room. I am sitting in the attic of our old house, the Old Soul, reading in the sunlight. I hear the ladybug before I see it. A little noise that echoes in an extended moment. *(A beat, then the lights change.)* A sunshower. I didn't know they could happen. I am small and Attlea is crawling. We are outside in the grass, under the sun, and I feel a raindrop. Then another, and then a whole shower. But the sun doesn't go away. It stays for an extended moment. I didn't know that could happen. *(A spiral staircase appears, and brings with it a soft glow of colorful light. Sophi looks at the stairs.)* It is time to go home.

the stairs

(Sophi winds slowly up the stairs when she is stopped by another rumble and tremor. Lights flicker.)

COUNTER-KING

(voice only) He's gone.

SOPHI

(Begins climbing again, faster and faster.) No. No. No no no no...*(Lights go out as she yells)* You're my father! That's who you are!

home

(Silence and half-light. Emory is shakily working on his card castle again. Sophi sits by what is presumably her father's bedside.)

SOPHI

(softly) That's who you are. And this *(indicates the box)* is who you were. But they don't cancel each other out. All of this is you. And—

ATTLEA & SOPHI

All the world is here. *(Attlea walks over to Emory and steadies his hand. For the first time, he sees her. Time is stopped and the Stars come forward to address the audience.)*

STAR 1

Here is what matters.

STAR 2

Here is what matters.

STAR 3

Here is what matters. When Father's time came, he joined the Earth.

STAR 1

A monument stood above him, aimed at the Sky.

STAR 2

It bore the usual information, and then a quotation.

STAR 3

"Instructions on Finding Me Now—"

STARS

"Look."

SOPHI

"Anywhere." Look. *(Sophi opens the box, and realizes that it is empty. Then she begins to look. She looks at her mother, who now holds in her hands the thing with feathers. She looks at Attlea, who is holding the can of laughter. She looks at Emory, whose steady right hand holds a shell. She looks back into the box, and smiles. She reaches her hand in…the lights fade.)*

end of play